CONTENTS

Words in **bold** can be found in the glossary on pages 30–31.

COOL EMERGENCY MACHINES!

Here are ten of the coolest emergency machines you'll ever see! But they're not just amazing to look at. They're cool because they are toweringly tall, super-sleek or truly tough.

Fire engines, police supercars, lifeboats, aircraft and military ambulances all help out during emergencies. They fight fires, chase criminals and rescue people in danger. They boast cool equipment, such as long ladders, powerful pumps and wide **tracks**.

TEN
FIRE ENGINES
EMERGENCY VEHICLES

Chris Oxlade

W
FRANKLIN WATTS
LONDON•SYDNEY

Franklin Watts
First published in Great Britain in 2017 by The Watts Publishing Group
Copyright © The Watts Publishing Group 2017

Credits
Series Editor: Amy Pimperton
Series Designer: Mo Choy Design Ltd.
Picture Researcher: Diana Morris
Picture credits: ARKTOS ® Developments Ltd: 5, 20, 21t, 21b, 27tl, 30. BMW: 18, 27cr. Jenny Bowden/
Dreamstime: 23t. Boykov/Shutterstock: front cover main, 1. Mario Burger: 13t. DOK-ING Ltd: 10c, 10b, 11t, 11c,
26cr. Fotografiche/Shutterstock: front cover bc. goodcat/Shutterstock: front cover crb. Antonio Gravante/
Shutterstock: front cover cl. Clarence Holmes Photography/Alamy: 12b, 26cl. Jasper Image/Shutterstock:
front cover tc. Kalewa/Shutterstock: 15t. Leonid Katskya/Dreamstime: 25b. Kietr/Shutterstock: front cover tr.
Phil King/Shutterstock: front cover cl. KMWEG: 4, 14, 15b, 26b, 31b. © Lamborghini: 16b, 17b, 27cl. Guiseppe
Malara/Dreamstime: 31t. Mandritou/Dreamstime: 13b. PA Archive/PAI: 2t, 22, 27tr. Pannarat Rattanakulsawad/
Shutterstock: front cover tl. Vladimir Rejda: 19, 29t. Rosenbauer Group: 6, 7t, 7b, 8, 9c, 9b, 26tl, 26tr. Scania
AB: 23c. Alex Schmidt/Shutterstock: front cover bl, 17t. Heather Snow/Dreamstime: 24, 27b. supergenijalac/
Shutterstock: front cover clb. Toa55134048720/Shutterstock: front cover br. Tupungato/Dreamstime: 25t.
welcomia/Shutterstock: front cover cr.
Every attempt has been made to clear copyright. Should there be any
inadvertent omission please apply to the publisher for rectification.

HB ISBN   978 1 4451 5510 4
PB ISBN   978 1 4451 5511 1

Printed in China

Franklin Watts
An imprint of
Hachette Children's Group
Part of The Watts Publishing Group
Carmelite House
50 Victoria Embankment
London EC4Y 0DZ

An Hachette UK Company
www.hachette.co.uk
www.franklinwatts.co.uk

Note to parents and teachers: Every effort has been made by the Publishers to ensure that the websites in
this book are suitable for children, that they are of the highest educational value, and that they contain
no inappropriate or offensive material. However, because of the nature of the Internet, it is impossible to
guarantee that the contents of these sites will not be altered. We strongly advise that Internet access is
supervised by a responsible adult.

Look out for the Fantastic 5 panels. Here you'll find out five fantastic facts about each vehicle.

FANTASTIC 5

TALL

Let's start with a super-tall machine. The AERIAL LADDER reaches high into the air to help fight fires and pluck people from danger.

An aerial ladder is a fire engine with a rescue cage on the end of a super-long ladder. Firefighters stand in the cage to spray water onto a fire or rescue people in danger. The *Rosenbauer Raptor* is used by firefighters in the USA.

FANTASTIC

ROSENBAUER RAPTOR

- **Length:** 12 metres
- **Ladder length:** 31 metres
- **Water tank:** 1,136 litres
- **Pumping power:** 5,680 litres per minute
- **Crew:** 6 (4 in the cage; 2 on the ground)

STABILISERS
Stabilisers are legs that stop the Raptor from toppling over. There is a stabiliser at each corner of the fire engine.

RESCUE CAGE
The rescue cage has operating controls in it and enough space for four firefighters.

RAPID

A CRASH TENDER only works around airport runways. These fire engines are always ready and waiting in case of accidents.

A crash tender rushes to the rescue when planes are forced to do **emergency landings** in case a fire starts on board. **Jet fuel** is very **flammable**, so the fire engine sprays foam to put out any flames. The *Rosenbauer Panther 8x8* is used by airport firefighters all over the world.

FLUGHAFEN DRESDEN

MAN

FOAM NOZZLE
The foam **nozzle** sprays a mixture of water and a special foam.

ROSENBAUER PANTHER 8x8

⚙ **Length:** 12 metres

⚙ **Top speed:** 135 kilometres per hour

⚙ **Pumping power:** 9,000 litres per minute

⚙ **Width:** 3 metres

⚙ **Crew:** 6

The STINGER
The stinger is a giant needle that can pierce a plane's side to shoot foam inside the aircraft.

CLEVER

Some emergency machines go where firefighters can't. A ROBOT FIREFIGHTING VEHICLE can get very close to fires to put out the flames.

What if an emergency scene is too dangerous for human firefighters? A fire may be too fierce, or there may be dangerous chemicals around. A robot firefighting vehicle, such as the *DOK-ING MVF-5*, is the answer. This mini, fireproof machine is operated by remote control.

DOZER BLADE

The metal dozer blade can push objects that weigh up to nine tonnes out of its way.

FANTASTIC ⑤

DOK-ING MVF-5

⚙ **Length:** 3.8 metres

⚙ **Weight:** 9.7 tonnes

⚙ **Top speed:** 12 kilometres per hour

⚙ **Water tank:** 2,200 litres

⚙ **Pumping power:** 2,000 litres per minute

GRIPPER

The gripper is a huge claw on the front of the robot. It is used to grab and drag objects away from danger.

POWERFUL

A cool FIREBOAT can tackle red-hot emergencies! These special boats help to fight fires on riverbanks, seafronts, ships and oil rigs.

This large Ranger 4200 fireboat is named *THREE FORTY THREE*. It is the **flagship** of the New York City Fire Department's **fleet**. It has lots of nozzles, called monitors, to spray water at fires. A powerful pump sucks water from under the boat and pushes it through the monitors.

FANTASTIC

5

THREE FORTY THREE

- ⚙ **Length:** 43 metres
- ⚙ **Weight:** 500 tonnes
- ⚙ **Top speed:** 34 kilometres per hour
- ⚙ **Pumping power:** 190,000 litres per minute
- ⚙ **Crew:** 7

COMMAND CENTRE
The control and command centre is where the captain and crew steer the boat and operate its equipment from.

WATER SALUTES
Three Forty Three's sister ship, Firefighter II, performs a water salute at a 4th of July celebration in the USA.

TOUGH

A tough MILITARY AMBULANCE carries injured soldiers to safety in **war zones** and other dangerous places.

The *KMW GFF 4* military ambulance has a heavy-duty chassis, or frame. Thick **armour** protects the crew from bullets or in case the ambulance hits an explosive **mine**. Its six big wheels have chunky tyres for good grip over the roughest ground.

RED CROSS

A red cross on a white background is the **symbol** for a **medical** vehicle. This sign shows that the ambulance is carrying injured people.

SAFETY CELL

A safety cell is a strong compartment in the rear of the ambulance. Inside are stretchers and first-aid equipment.

FANTASTIC

⑤

KMW GFF 4

⚙ **Length:** 8 metres

⚙ **Weight:** 25 tonnes

⚙ **Top speed:** 90 kilometres per hour

⚙ **Engine power:** 450 **horsepower**

⚙ **Width:** 2.5 metres

SUPER-SLEEK

Some police officers are very lucky. They get to drive the fastest police cars! The luckiest of all get to drive POLICE SQUAD SUPERCARS.

Police officers sometimes need to drive fast to chase speedy suspects trying to escape. This sleek squad car is the incredible *LAMBORGHINI HURACÁN LP610-4 POLIZIA*. Lamborghini – one of Italy's most famous supercar makers – gave this one-off car to the Italian police force as a gift.

LIGHT BAR

A warning light bar sits on a police car's roof. The warning lights have super-bright blue and red LEDs.

FANTASTIC 5

LAMBORGHINI HURACÁN LP610-4 POLIZIA

- ⚙ **Length:** 4.5 metres
- ⚙ **Top speed:** 323 kilometres per hour
- ⚙ **Engine power:** 602 horsepower
- ⚙ **Width:** 1.9 metres
- ⚙ **Engine size:** 5.2 litres

STREAMLINED BODY

The car's streamlined body has a smooth shape. This allows it to cut through the air at top speed.

SUPER-FAST

A POLICE SUPERBIKE is a super-fast road motorcycle. Nobody can escape a police officer riding one of these!

Superbikes are the fastest road motorcycles on the planet. They are lightweight but have hugely powerful engines, and smooth, streamlined bodies that get them up to top speed in a flash! The lightning-fast *BMW S1000RR* (known as the 'RR') is BMW's fastest motorcycle. It is ridden by police traffic officers in the USA and the UK.

RR BIKES
The first RR bikes were ridden by Rubén 'Spiderman' Xaus in the 2009 Superbike World Championships, for the BMW Motorrad team.

ABS
The ABS (Anti-lock Braking System) helps a rider keep control when breaking at high speed or in slippery conditions.

FANTASTIC

5

BMW S1000RR

- **Length:** 2 metres
- **Weight:** 183 kilogrammes
- **Top speed:** Over 200 kilometres per hour
- **Engine power:** 193 horsepower
- **Engine size:** 1 litre

RUGGED

People have accidents and get stuck in all sorts of hard-to-reach places. An ALL-TERRAIN RESCUE VEHICLE is ready to get them out of trouble.

All-terrain vehicles can travel across almost anything. Some, like the *ARKTOS® **AMPHIBIOUS** CRAFT*, can travel over land and through water! The ARKTOS® is made up of two vehicles with tracks. The vehicles are linked together. It works in icy **Arctic** waters. It can even climb out of the water onto **ice floes**.

FANTASTIC

5

ARKTOS® AMPHIBIOUS CRAFT

- ⚙ **Length:** 15 metres
- ⚙ **Weight:** 32 tonnes
- ⚙ **Top speed:** 12 kilometres per hour
- ⚙ **Rescue capacity:** Up to 52 people
- ⚙ **Operating conditions:** All-weather

WATERTIGHT HULL

The machine has an air-filled, watertight hull that keeps water out and stops the craft from sinking.

TRACKS

The caterpillar tracks push the vehicle along in water and on land. They spread the vehicle's weight to stop it getting stuck in mud or breaking thin ice.

UNSINKABLE

A fearless LIFEBOAT crew race to the rescue out at sea, even in the stormiest weather.

This *RNLI SHANNON CLASS LIFEBOAT* is (almost) unsinkable. It has a tough steel hull, and when all the watertight hatches, windows and doors are shut, water can't get in. It's also self-righting, which means that if the lifeboar gets knocked over by a monster wave, it flips back up again.

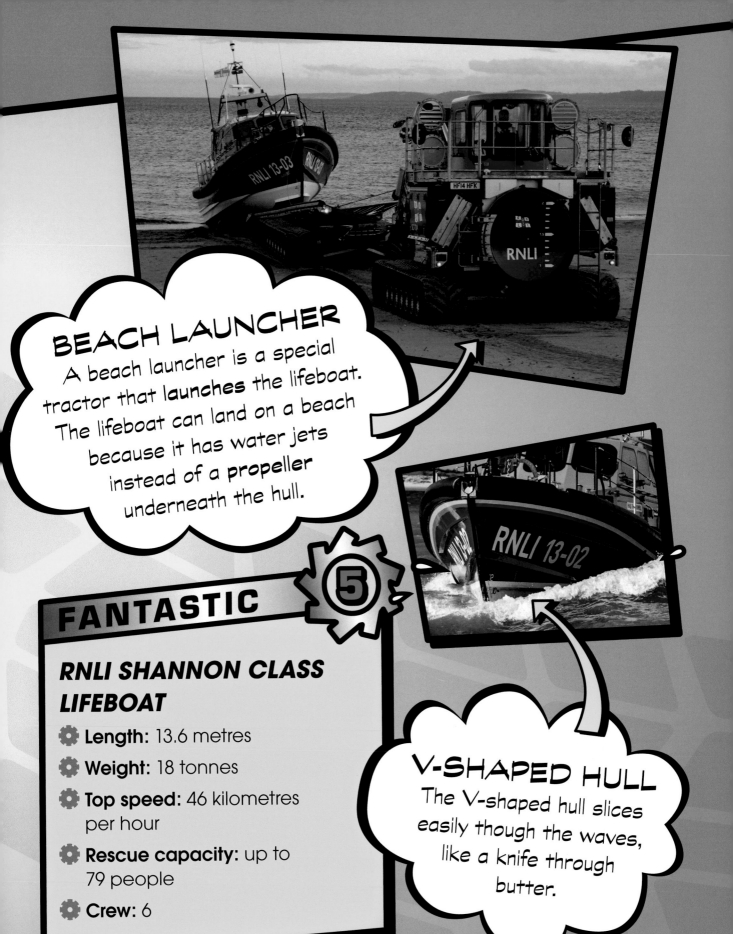

BEACH LAUNCHER

A beach launcher is a special tractor that launches the lifeboat. The lifeboat can land on a beach because it has water jets instead of a **propeller** underneath the hull.

5

FANTASTIC

RNLI SHANNON CLASS LIFEBOAT

⚙ **Length:** 13.6 metres

⚙ **Weight:** 18 tonnes

⚙ **Top speed:** 46 kilometres per hour

⚙ **Rescue capacity:** up to 79 people

⚙ **Crew:** 6

V-SHAPED HULL

The V-shaped hull slices easily though the waves, like a knife through butter.

ACROBATIC

It's often tricky for a fire engine to get close to forest fires. So firefighters call in FIREFIGHTING AIRCRAFT to dump water on the flames.

A firefighting aircraft carries water in special tanks. To fill its tanks, the *BOMBARDIER 415* skims across a lake or sea at high speed, scooping up water. It takes a skilled pilot to pull off this tricky move! It empties its tanks of water as it flies over the fire.

FANTASTIC

5

BOMBARDIER 415

- ⚙ **Length:** 20 metres
- ⚙ **Wingspan:** 29 metres
- ⚙ **Top speed:** 333 kilometres per hour
- ⚙ **Water tank:** 6,000 litres
- ⚙ **Nickname:** 'Superscooper'

SCOOP
The scoop collects water as the plane skims along. It takes just 12 seconds to fill the tanks.

FLOATS
Two air-filled floats on the wings stop them dipping into the water as the plane scoops.

TEN MORE COOL FACTS

TALL: The ***Rosenbauer Raptor*** takes just 60 seconds to extend its stabilisers and raise its ladder to its full height!

RAPID: *The **Rosenbauer Panther 8x8*** tackles airport emergencies in 81 countries around the world.

CLEVER: The ***DOK-ING MVF-5*** is tough enough to keep on working even if it runs over a mine!

POWERFUL: ***Three Forty Three*** cost $27 million (£22 million)! The FDNY has another identical boat called ***Fire Fighter II***.

TOUGH: ***KMW GFF 4*** is nicknamed 'Grizzly' after a very large and dangerous type of brown bear.

SUPER-SLEEK: The Italian police force once had a Lamborghini Gallardo, but an officer crashed it into a line of parked cars! The **Lamborghini Huracán LP610-4** replaced the Gallardo.

SUPER-FAST: The **BMW S1000RR** can go from 0–60 kilometres per hour in 2.6 seconds.

RUGGED: The **ARKTOS® Amphibious Craft** can work in temperatures as low as 50° Celsius.

UNSINKABLE: It costs £2.2 million to run a **RNLI Shannon Class** lifeboat for one year.

ACROBATIC: The **Bombardier 415** can scoop up water that is only two metres deep. That means the aircraft is only two metres from the ground when performing this move!

STACK UP THOSE STATS!

Here are the ten cool machines with all their stats and a few more. Which is your favourite machine?

	Rosenbauer Raptor	Rosenbauer Panther 8x8	DOK-ING MVF-5	Three Forty Three	KMW GFF 4
Length	12 metres	12 metres	3.8 metres	43 metres	8 metres
Top speed		135 kph	12 kph	34 kph	90 kph
Weight		52 tonnes	9.7 tonnes	500 tonnes	25 tonnes
Width	2.5 metres	3 metres	2.2 metres	11 metres	2.5 metres
Crew	6	6	0	7	11
Pumping power	5,680 lpm	9,000 lpm	2,000 lpm	190,000 lpm	
Engine power	450 hp	1,400 hp	250 hp		450 hp
Water tank	1,136 litres	19,000 litres	2,200 litres		
Rescue capacity					10 people
Engine size					
Nickname					Grizzly
Ladder length	31 metres				
Operating conditions					

Rosenbauer Panther 8x8 can hold the most water.

Three Forty Three is the longest machine.

QUIZ

1 What are stabiliser legs on an aerial ladder?

2 On which emergency vehicle would you find a stinger?

3 Which machine has a giant claw on its front?

4 What is a monitor?

5 What symbol shows that a vehicle is an ambulance?

BMW SR1000RR is the lightest machine.

Bombardier 415 is the fastest machine.

Lamborghini Huracán LP610-4 Polizia	BMW S1000RR	Arktos ® Amphibious Craft	RNLI Shannon Class Lifeboat	Bombardier 415
4.5 metres	2 metres	15 metres	13.6 metres	20 metres
323 kph	200+ kph	12 kph	46 kph	333 kph
1.5 tonnes	183 kilogrammes	32 tonnes	18 tonnes	13 tonnes
1.9 metres			4.5 metres	29 metres (wingspan)
	1		6	2
602 hp	193 hp		650 hp	
				6,000 litres
		52 people	79 people	8
5.2 litres	1 litre		13 litres	
				Superscooper
		All weather	All weather	

kph = kilometres per hour   lpm = litres per minute   hp = horsepower

6 What sort of vehicle does the company Lamborghini make?

7 What do the letters ABS stand for?

8 Which vehicle can tackle icy water?

9 What sort of rescue boat can flip itself the right way up?

10 How long does it take a Bombardier 415 to fill its water tanks?

GLOSSARY

4th of July a special holiday, also known as Independence Day, that is celebrated in the USA

amphibious something at home in water and on land

Arctic the area of the world around the North Pole

armour strong metal plates that protect against bullets or other weapons

emergency landing when a plane makes an unscheduled landing due to unexpected circumstances, such as a faulty engine

flagship the most important or biggest ship in a fleet

flammable easily set on fire

fleet a group of ships

horsepower a measure of how much power an engine produces

hull the main part of a boat or ship that sits in the water

ice floe a sheet of ice floating on the sea

jet fuel the special fuel used in jet engines

launch to put a boat or ship in the water

LED short for light emiting diode; a type of lightbulb

medical to do with medicine

mine a bomb hidden underground

nozzle a narrow hole at the end of a tube that liquid squirts through

Further Information

WEBSITES:

http://www.rosenbauer.co.uk
Lots of pictures and facts about Rosenbauer's firefighting machines, including airport crash tenders.

http://marine1fdny.com/
Information about the FDNY firefighting boats.
https:// www.lamborghini.com/en-en/models/huracan
Cool pictures and stats on the Huracán supercar.

BOOKS
Busy Builders: Fire Station by Chris Oxlade (Templar)
Emergency Vehicles: Fire Truck by Chris Oxlade (QED Publishing)
Emergency Vehicles: Fire Rescue by Deborah Chancellor (Franklin Watts)

PLACES TO VISIT

Royal National Lifeboat Institution stations
You can visit many of the RNLI's lifeboat stations to see the lifeboats and meet the crews
https://rnli.org/find-my-nearest/lifeboat-stations

The National Emergency Services Museum
This museum in Sheffield, South Yorkshire, has historic fire engines and exhibits
http://www.firepolicemuseum.org.uk

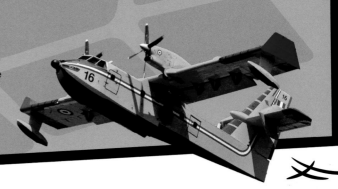

oil rig a tower built at sea that is used to drill into the seabed for oil

propeller a fan-like machine that spins around and pushes water or air along

symbol a shape that stands for something else

track a loop of metal plates that that some vehicles have instead of wheels

war zone a place where a war is being fought

water salute when huge jets of water are sprayed during a ceremony or a celebration

INDEX

QUIZ ANSWERS
1 Stabiliser legs stop an aerial ladder toppling over.
2 A stinger can be found on an airport crash tender.
3 The *DOK-ING MVF-5* robot firefighting vehicle has a giant claw.
4 A monitor is a nozzle that sprays water.
5 A red cross on a white background shows a vehicle is an ambulance. (In some countries the symbol is a red crescent.)
6 Lamborghini make supercars.
7 ABS stands for **A**nti-lock **B**raking **S**ystem.
8 An all-terrain amphibious craft can tackle icy water.
9 The *RNLI Shannon CLass Lifeboat* can flip itself the right way up if powerful waves knock it over.
10 It takes a *Bombardier 415* 12 seconds to fill its water tanks.